Julia Esther Arellano
DOB: 02/13/54
Sex: F   Race: White/Hisp
Height: 5'2"   Weight: 120 lbs
Hair: Brown   Eyes: Hazel

Alias: Julia Esther Urbina or Julia Esther Carrillo Alonso.

Elizabeth M. Arellano
Missing: 07/23/91   Age Now: 10 yr
Missing From: Manitoba, CN
DOB: 02/26/85   Age Disap: 6 yr
Sex: F   Race: White/Hisp
Height: 3'5"   Weight: 44 lbs
Hair: Brown   Eyes: Blue

Abducted by mother, Julia Esther Arellano.

Walter Ricardo Arellano
Missing: 07/23/91   Age Now: 14 yr
Missing From: Manitoba, CN
DOB: 10/7/81   Age Disap: 9 yr
Sex: M   Race: White/Hisp
Height: 4'5"   Weight: 73 lbs
Hair: Brown   Eyes: Brown

Wears glasses, scar on right eyebrow. Abducted by mother, Julia Esther Arellano.

Ashley Marie Dalton
Missing: 11/13/94   Age Now: 5 yr
Missing From: Richmond, VA
DOB: 07/12/90   Age Disap: 4 yr
Sex: F   Race: White
Height: 3'7"   Weight: 48 lbs
Hair: Brown   Eyes: Blue

Abducted by mother, Tara Marie Gomes.

Tara Marie Gomes
DOB: 10/21/71
Sex: F   Race: White/Hisp
Height: 5'6"   Weight: 160 lbs
Hair: Brown   Eyes: Hazel

Facial scars, may walk with a limp. May be wearing glasses. Front teeth crowded together.

Adel Bjiouat
Missing: 07/6/94   Age Now: 7 yr
Missing From: Raytown, MO
DOB: 12/17/87   Age Disap: 6 yr
Sex: M   Race: White
Height: 4'0"   Weight: 50 lbs
Hair: Black   Eyes: Brown

Nickname is Del. Abducted by father, Khalid Bjiouat.

Khalid Bjiouat
DOB: 12/4/63
Sex: M   Race: White
Height: 6'2""   Weight: 170 lbs
Hair: Black   Eyes: Brown
Has a moustache, possibly a goatee.

DOB:
Sex: F   Race: White
Height: 5'9"   Weight: 120 lbs
Hair: Blonde   Eyes: Green

Stephanie Marie Schild
Missing: 10/02/89   Age Now: 9 yr
Missing From: Cincinnati, OH
DOB: 11/2/86   Age Disap: 2 yr
Sex: F   Race: White
Height: 2'10"   Weight: 35 lbs
Hair: Blonde   Eyes: Blue

Hair brownish-blonde. Abducted by mother, Sharon Francis Schild.

Oscar Oblajura Emeasoba
Missing: 08/17/92   Age Now: 4 yr
Missing From: Silver Spring, MD
DOB: 03/20/91   Age Disap: 17 mo
Sex: M   Race: Black
Height: 2'0"   Weight: 28 lbs
Hair: Black   Eyes: Brown

Small black birthmark on upper leg. Abducted by father, Augustine Emeosoba.

Augustine Okechuckwu Emeasoba
DOB: 12/24/42
Sex: M   Race: Black
Height: 5'8"   Weight: 200 lbs
Hair: Black/grey   Eyes: Brown

Large mouth & nose, scars on hands and feet.

Robert Edward Maloney
Missing: 03/1/94   Age Now: 12 yr
Missing From: San Jose, CA
DOB: 03/04/83   Age Disap: 11 yr
Sex: M   Race: White/Hisp
Height: 5'0"   Weight: 90 lbs
Hair: Blonde   Eyes: Green

May be in company of non-custodial father.

Kali Ann Poulton
Missing: 05/23/94   Age Now: 6 yr
Missing From: East Rochester, NY
DOB: 09/20/89   Age Disap: 4 yr
Sex: F   Race: White
Height: 4'0"   Weight: 40 lbs
Hair: Blonde   Eyes: Blue

Small light brown moles on each side of face by lower jaw. Pierced ears.

Civil War Era
ACTIVITY BOOK

Author	Linda Milliken
Editor	Kathy Rogers
Design	Mary Jo Keller
Illustrator	Barb Lorseyedi

© 1996 **EDUPRESS** • P.O. Box 883 • Dana Point, CA 92629
ISBN 1-56472-108-6
Printed in USA

Table of Contents

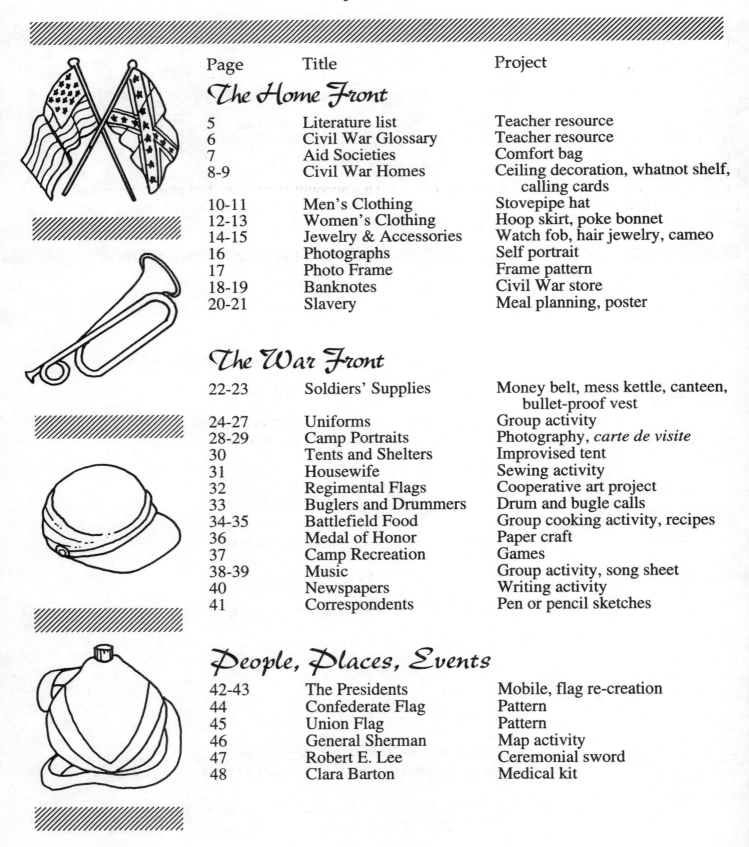

Literature List

- **The Tin Heart**
by Karen Ackerman;
Macmillan 1990. (1-3)
Even the Civil War cannot split the
friendship of two girls from families of
different sides.

- **Mountain Boy**
by Anna Catherine Josephs;
Raintree LB 1985. (1-3)
The true story of a 14-year-old boy who led
Union soldiers through the South Carolina
mountains.

- **Jefferson Davis**
by Zachary Kent;
Childrens LB 1993. (3-5)
The story of the American statesman who
was president of the Confederacy from 1861
to 1865.

- **The Story of Sherman's March to the Sea**
by Zachary Kent;
Childrens LB 1987. (3-6)
The profile of the Union general in the Civil
War and his destructive march from Atlanta
to the sea.

- **The Story of the Monitor and the
Merrimac**
by Conrad R. Stein;
Childrens LB 1983. (3-6)
The story of the two Civil War ships and
their fateful encounter.

- **The Story of the Surrender at Appomattox
Court House**
by Zachary Kent;
Childrens LB 1988. (3-5)
The end of the Civil War and the
momentous meeting between Lee and Grant.

- **Clara Barton: Healing the Wounds**
by Cathy E. Dubowski;
Silver LB 1991. (4-7)
The story of the Civil War nurse and teacher
who started the American Red Cross.

- **Lincoln: A Photobiography**
by Russell Freedman;
Houghton 1987. (4-8)
A pictorial look at the 16th president. A
Newbery Medal winner.

- **Behind the Blue and Gray: The Soldier's
Life in the Civil War**
by Delia Ray;
Dutton 1991. (4-7)
This account re-creates the behind-the-front
lives of both Union and Confederate
soldiers.

- **Robert E. Lee**
by Nathan Aaseng;
Lerner LB 1991. (4-6)
A biography of the great leader of the South
during the Civil War.

- **Behind the Lines: A Sourcebook on the
Civil War**
by Carter Smith, ed;
Millbrook LB 1993. (5-8)
A visual sourcebook describing life on the
home front and in the army camps.

- **A Month of Seven Days**
by Shirley Climo;
Harper LB 1987. (5-7)
Driven from her home by a Yankee captain,
12-year-old Zoe learns that not all bluecoats
need be enemies.

- **Across Five Aprils**
by Irene Hunt;
Silver Burdett 1993. (6-8)
A family is divided when one brother joins
the Union forces, and the other the
Confederacy.

- **Rifles for Watie**
by Harold Keith;
Harper LB 1991. (6-8)
Life of a Union soldier and spy fighting the
Civil War in the West. Newbery Medal
winner, 1958.

Civil War Glossary

abolitionist—a person who worked to end slavery in the United States

artillery—a branch of the armed forces that operates large mounted guns, too heavy to carry; also, the guns themselves

bayonet—a long, narrow-bladed knife designed to fit on the end of a rifle barrel and to be used in hand-to-hand combat

blockade—to prevent the entry and exit of ships from a harbor

carte de visite—an early type of photograph in which the image was printed from a glass negative onto a paper card

casualty—a soldier, who, during a battle, is killed, wounded, captured, or missing in action

cavalry—a branch of the army trained to fight on horseback

Confederate States of America—the alliance of eleven southern states that withdrew from the United States in 1860 and 1861: Alabama, Arkansas, Florida, Georgia, Louisiana, Mississippi, North Carolina, South Carolina, Tennessee, Texas, and Virginia; also referred to as the Confederacy

contraband—a slave who escaped to or was brought into Union lines

Democrat—a member of the political party that supported slavery and believed states should control their own affairs without interference from the national government

draft—the government's selection of citizens for a required period of military service

emancipate—to free from slavery

Emancipation Proclamation—an act issued by President Lincoln in 1862 that freed all slaves in the rebel states

enlist—to join the armed services

Federal—having to do with the union of states that recognized the authority of the United States government based in Washington, D.C.

infantry—a branch of the army made up of units trained to fight on foot

rebel—another term for a Confederate soldier or a civilian supporter of the Confederacy

Union—another name for the United States of America, used especially during the Civil War

Yankee—another name for a Northerner

Aid Societies

Historical Aid

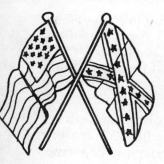

People on the Union home front rallied to form *aid societies* that assisted in providing the many needs of the soldiers on the battle front. Aid society members gathered canned and dried food, knitted socks, and made uniforms and underwear. They made bandages from any available material. They sold everything from baked goods to machinery to raise money to finance the war effort.

The food and clothing assembled were used to fill "comfort bags," which were sent to the troops. Although they didn't know who would receive the comfort bag, aid society members and their children often added a personal note, encouraging the soldier and sending news from the home front.

Project

Prepare a "comfort bag" to send to a soldier on the battle front.

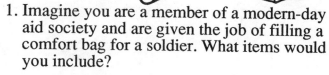

Materials
- Paper lunch bags
- Magazines
- Scissors
- Items from home
- Paper, pencils

Directions

1. Imagine you are a member of a modern-day aid society and are given the job of filling a comfort bag for a soldier. What items would you include?

2. Look through magazines and cut out pictures of things you would send. Add items brought from home. Write a personal note of encouragement and share some hometown news.

3. Meet in small discussion groups to share the contents of the comfort bag with group members. Explain the reason for your choices. Evaluate the choices of others.

Civil War Homes

Historical Aid

By the time of the Civil War homes were becoming modern. Kitchens were separate from the dining room, with a cookstove and oven. The dining room became an important gathering place for the family. The parlor, similar to a living room, was another room where the family gathered for entertaining or for recreation. Parlors were often furnished with a large central table where the family worked or read together in the evenings.

Floors were covered with carpet, matting, or painted oilcloth. Ceilings were often elaborately decorated. Houses were lit with candles or kerosene lamps. It was common for each family member to have a separate bedroom.

Ceilings

Ceilings in Civil War homes might be painted, stencilled, papered, or covered with decorated tin sheets or painted linen. Create a ceiling design to cover the classroom ceiling.

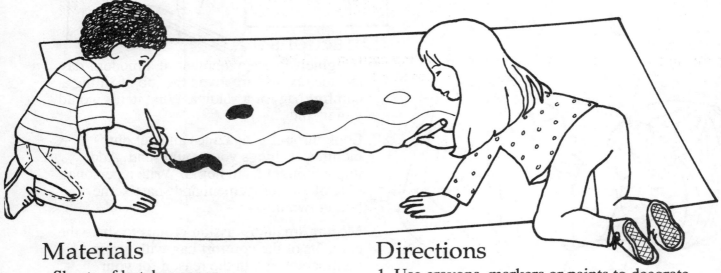

Materials

- Sheets of butcher paper
- Crayons, markers, or tempera paint and brushes
- Double-sided tape

Directions

1. Use crayons, markers or paints to decorate sheets of butcher paper with patterns.

2. Use double-sided tape to fasten paper to classroom ceiling.

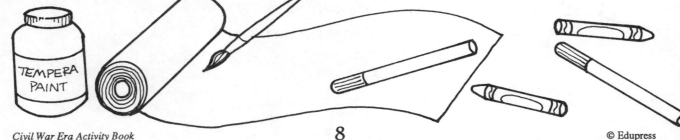

Civil War Homes

Whatnot Shelf

A fixture in Civil War parlors was the whatnot, a piece of furniture made of graduated open shelves to hold photographs, bric-a-brac, and family souvenirs.

Materials

• Bookshelf or table
• Tablecloth (optional)

Directions

1. Designate a bookshelf area or set aside a table covered with a tablecloth.

2. Bring items from home that may be put on the shelf. Include natural items such as shells and rocks.

Calling Cards

Visitors to a Civil War home might leave a calling card on the table in the entrance hall. These cards were often decorated and were printed with the caller's name. In some homes, there was a xylophone in the hall that was used to announce visitors and household events such as mealtimes. Specific tunes might be used to designate individual visitors or announcements.

Materials

• Unlined index cards, cut in half
• Crayons or markers
• Fine-tipped marker
• Xylophone

Directions

1. Use fine-tipped marker to write name on index card.

2. Decorate card with markers or crayons.

3. Compose a short tune on the xylophone.

4. Take turns paying calls, leaving cards and announcing your arrival with a xylophone tune!

Men's Clothing

Historical Aid

By the time of the Civil War, great changes had taken place in clothing styles and construction. The invention of the sewing machine meant that clothes could be sold ready-made in stores. Standardized sewing patterns were sold for home use.

Styles for men were less elaborate than they had been in earlier times. Men in the city wore dark suits with white shirts and ties. Stovepipe hats were popular, and many men carried pocket watches with chains and fobs. For home wear, men had loose jackets called smoking jackets.

Project

Dress like a business man living in Civil War times.

Materials

- Man's dress jacket
- Wide black ribbon or bow tie
- White dress shirt
- Stovepipe hat (following page)
- Watch chain and fob (page 14)

Directions

1. Dress in suggested clothing.
2. Compare Civil War dress to the way men dress today.

Men's Clothing

Stovepipe Hat

The stovepipe hat was a top hat that was popular throughout most of the 19th century. It could be made of many materials, from beaver skin to silk.

Materials

- Black poster board
- Black construction paper
- Scissors
- Tape

Directions

1. Cut a 12-inch (30 cm) circle from poster board to form base of hat.

2. Cut center out of the poster board circle, leaving 2 inches (5 cm) for brim.

3. Cut a 12 x 27-inch (30 x 69 cm) rectangle of black construction paper for crown. Roll to form a column, adjusting to fit inside hat brim. Tape together.

4. Cut 1-inch (2.54 cm) slashes at 1-inch (2.54 cm) intervals around bottom of column. Fold up.

5. Tape folded tabs to under side of brim to form hat crown.

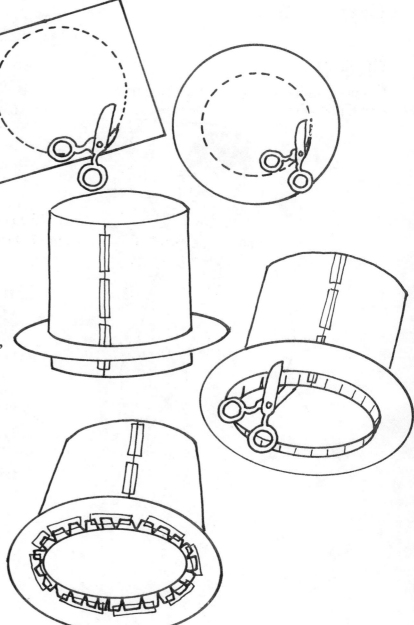

Women's Clothing

Historical Aid

Clothing for women in Civil War times could be very elaborate. Dresses were worn over large hoop skirts that were sometimes so wide that a woman might have difficulty going through doors. Several layers of petticoats were worn under the skirt. Women also wore corsets, which bound their waists to unnaturally small sizes. Women accessorized their ensembles with gloves, jewelry, and elaborate hats.

Many types of fabric were used for clothing, but cotton was the most common. Manufacturing methods were so improved that cotton fabrics could have many different textures, colors, and prints.

Project

Create a hoop skirt to be worn as part of a Civil War ensemble.

Materials

- Hula hoop
- Measuring tape
- Fabric
- Needle, thread
- Elastic
- Long, full skirt
- Hat (following page)
- Gloves

Directions

1. Measure circumference of hula hoop. Cut fabric to that length, adding 2 inches (5 cm).

2. Sew ends of fabric together. Fold over top edge 1 inch (2.54 cm) to form casing and insert elastic. Wrap bottom edge up over hula hoop and sew into place.

3. Wear long skirt over hoop skirt and add accessories.

4. Discuss the difference between Civil War clothing and the dresses of today.

Women's Clothing

Poke Bonnet

Poke bonnets were one type of hat worn by women in Civil War times. They were often elaborately decorated with ribbons, flowers, and feathers.

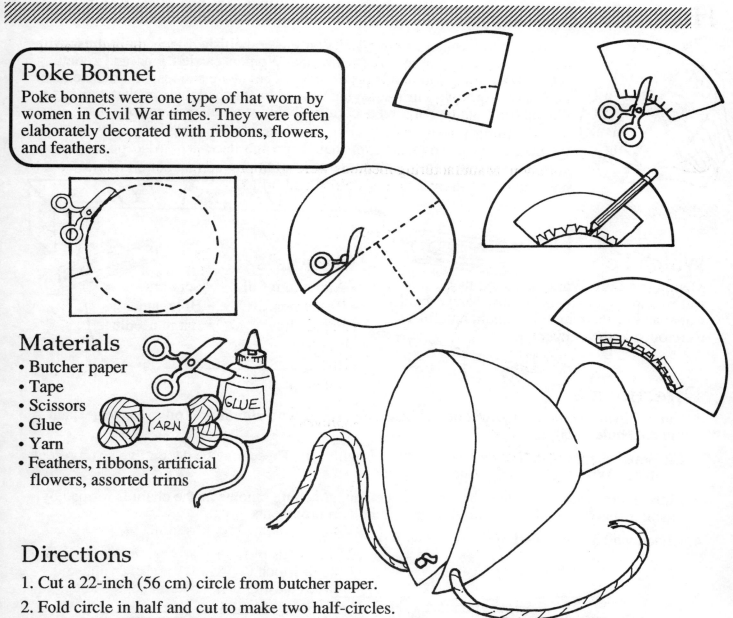

Materials
- Butcher paper
- Tape
- Scissors
- Glue
- Yarn
- Feathers, ribbons, artificial flowers, assorted trims

Directions

1. Cut a 22-inch (56 cm) circle from butcher paper.

2. Fold circle in half and cut to make two half-circles.

3. Cut one of half-circles in half again. Discard one section. Cut remaining quarter-circle as shown in diagram.

4. Make 1-inch (2.54 cm) slashes at intervals as shown. Fold back.

5. Lay quarter-circle on top of half-circle as shown and trace a curved cutting line. Cut away excess paper.

6. Tape folded edges of quarter-circle along cut edge of half-circle, curving larger piece to make a brim.

7. Cut holes and insert lengths of yarn to tie hat under chin.

8. Decorate bonnet by gluing on selected trims.

Jewelry & Accessories

Historical Aid

Men and women of the Civil War era embellished their daily dress with jewelry and other types of ornaments. Women carried fans and reticules, which were similar to handbags of today. They wore snoods, or crocheted hair nets, to cover their hair during the day. Men attached their pocket watches to chains from which dangled decorative baubles or charms, called fobs.

Mourning jewelry of all kinds was very fashionable, often made of jet (polished coal), wood, or even hair from the deceased. Also popular were cameos, set into rings, necklaces and earrings.

Watch Fob

Men in the Civil War era carried their watches in a special pocket just below the waistband of their suit. The chain and fobs were outside the pocket.

Materials

- Aluminum foil
- Poster board
- Paper clips
- Scissors
- Hole punch
- Large needle

Directions

1. Cut a 2-inch (5 cm) circle from poster board and cover with aluminum foil to make a watch. Punch a hole in circle.

2. Cut small shapes from poster board and cover with foil. These may be decorative or represent an object. With needle, poke a hole in each one.

3. Link several paper clips together to form a chain, attaching cutouts as the chain is formed by pushing sharp end of paper clip through the hole in ornaments.

4. Attach watch to one end of the chain with paper clip.

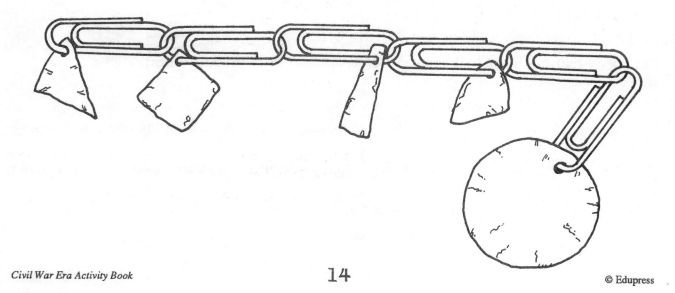

Jewelry & Accessories

Hair Jewelry

Human hair, woven and braided into necklaces, bracelets, earrings, and watch chains, served as mementoes of friends and relatives who had died. Sometimes hair from several family members was interwoven.

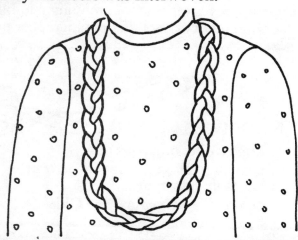

Materials

• Yarn in various colors

Directions

1. Cut several strands of yarn, all the same color or in various colors.

2. Experiment with weaving and braiding to find a pleasing pattern.

3. Fashion a bracelet or necklace from the braided length of yarn.

Cameos

A cameo is a gem carved with a figure raised in relief.

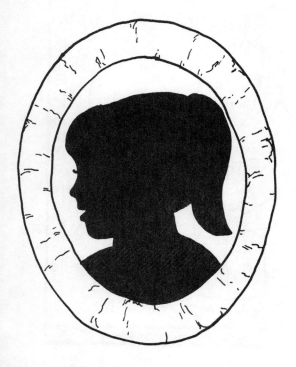

Materials

• Poster board oval, 3 inches (7.5 cm) long
• Aluminum foil
• Construction paper oval, slightly smaller than poster board
• White construction paper
• Pencil
• Scissors
• Tacky glue
• Pin back

Directions

1. Cover poster board oval with aluminum foil.

2. Glue construction paper oval to foil-covered oval.

3. Draw the outline of a face to fit inside construction paper oval. Cut out and glue to construction paper.

4. Glue pin back to back side of foil-covered oval.

Photographs

Historical Aid

When the war began in 1861, photography had been in existence only twenty-two years. Thousands of newly-enlisted soldiers and volunteers with "war fever" rushed to have their portraits taken. They donned whatever clothing and weapons they had available without waiting for their official uniforms to be issued. The poses often looked stiff, the faces expressionless. This was due, in part, to the ten second exposure time and the fact that their head was placed in metal clamps to prevent them from moving and blurring the picture. To give the illusion of an outdoor shot, the photographer painted backdrops featuring outdoor scenes.

Project

Create a self-portrait of a newly-enlisted Civil War soldier.

Materials

- Frame (following page)
- Personal photograph or self-portrait, preferably unsmiling
- Scissors   • Crayons   • Glue

Directions

1. Reproduce the picture frame.

2. Use crayons to create a landscape inside the frame and color the frame itself.

3. Cut yourself out of a photograph and glue it in the frame. If a photograph is unavailable, create a self-portrait.

4. Feature all the framed "photographs" in a classroom display.

Banknotes

Historical Aid

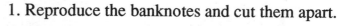

The banking system was chaotic throughout the North and South. Every state, many towns, banks, and even stores, issued their own currency. To finance the war effort, the South issued Federal bonds—loans in the form of paper money—that the government promised to repay, with interest, after the war was won. The debt was never repaid.

By 1865 inflation reached nine thousand percent. A Confederate "dollar" was worth barely more than a penny. Small fish sold for twenty dollars, chickens were ten dollars each. A Union private was paid $13 a month. A Confederate got $2 less. Bonuses were paid for enlisting and re-enlisting.

Project

Set up a Civil War store and spend paper currency.

Materials

- Banknotes (following page)
- Plastic food
- Food pictures cut from magazines

Directions

1. Reproduce the banknotes and cut them apart.

2. Set up a Civil War store with plastic food items and pictures of food cut from magazines.

3. Price the items in the store. Keep in mind the inflation of the era.

4. Decide which class members are bankers, shopkeepers, Union and Confederate soldiers. Determine how long the soldiers have served in the army and whether or not they deserve a bonus for re-enlisting.

5. Bankers pay each soldier the amount due.

6. Go shopping with the earned pay. Return everything to the store and assign different roles.

Slavery

Historical Aid

The issue of slavery was one of the causes of the Civil War. *Abolitionists* were people who felt that slavery should be ended. The life of a slave was completely controlled by his owner. There was no legal way for slaves to marry, and it was very common for families to be split up. It was against the law to educate slaves.

The conditions under which slaves lived varied widely. Some lived in the master's house, but many were housed in drafty, poorly furnished cabins. A slave might have only a bed of straw with a single blanket. A typical food allowance for one week might consist of three pounds of bacon and six quarts of cornmeal. Some slaves found the time to supplement their diet by growing vegetables or catching fish.

Project

Create menus for one week utilizing the normal food allowance for one slave.

Materials

- Cookbooks
- Paper
- Pencil
- Ingredients, utensils for one recipe (See Directions #3)

Directions

1. As a class, determine an exact food allotment for each person, including any extra food items that a slave might have available (see Historical Aid).

2. Look for recipes that use these food items, and plan a set of menus for one week.

3. Choose one recipe and prepare it.

Slavery

There were many people in the North and South who risked their lives trying to help slaves escape from their owners. Some were white abolitionists and some were free blacks. A religious group named the Society of Friends, or Quakers, began to help slaves escape as early as 1786. By 1860, an elaborate system called the underground railroad was well established. The "railroad" was actually a system of escape routes through "depots," or safe houses.

At these locations, families were willing to hide runaway slaves, feed and clothe them as necessary, and help them on their way to the next safe stop along their escape route. The ultimate destination was usually Canada, where blacks could work freely and could vote. Operators of the underground railroad sometimes used advertisements in newspapers to let prospective "riders" know of their existence.

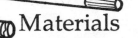

Project

Design a poster to advertise the operation of an underground railroad.

Materials

- Poster board
- Markers or crayons
- Newspaper or magazine advertisements

Directions

1. Study advertisements and brainstorm ideas for ways of describing the underground railroad in advertising terms.

2. Use poster board and markers or crayons to design ads.

3. Post finished advertisements in a bulletin board.

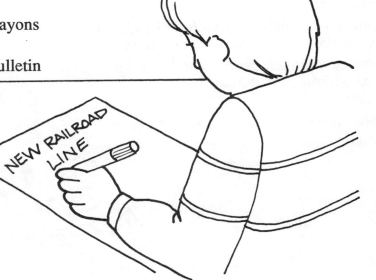

Sample advertisement appearing in a Chicago newspaper in 1844—
The improved and splendid Locomotives, Clarkson and Lundy, with their trains fitted up in the best style of accommodation for passengers, will run their regular trips during the present season...Gentlemen and Ladies, who may wish to improve their health or circumstances, by a northern tour, are respectfully invited to give us their patronage.

Soldiers' Supplies

Historical Aid

The call to arms and initial excitement of the war sent thousands of men shopping for their own supplies. Newspapers tempted new recruits with advertisements featuring the latest inventions and gadgets intended to make life on the war front more convenient.

Pocketed belts, bullet-proof vests, mess kettles, and even a portable nine-pound stove (cost: $6) were among the supplies offered for sale. Once purchased, they did not last long. Long hours of marching and difficult conditions forced soldiers to abandon these "luxuries." A bedroll, knapsack, and canteen were the only items a soldier could realistically carry.

Project

Construct some of the supplies sold through newspaper advertisements at the outset of the Civil War.

Directions

1. Reproduce the project page. Cut apart the project cards.

2. Discuss each project. Select one to complete. Provide additional materials, where indicated.

3. Display the projects and demonstrate the use of each one.

Materials

• Project page, following
• Materials as listed for each project
• Scissors
• Glue
• Stapler

Soldiers' Supplies

Money Belt

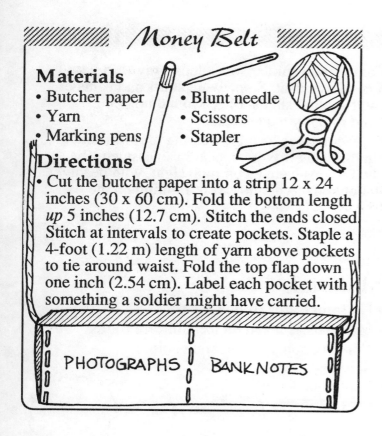

Materials
- Butcher paper
- Yarn
- Marking pens
- Blunt needle
- Scissors
- Stapler

Directions
- Cut the butcher paper into a strip 12 x 24 inches (30 x 60 cm). Fold the bottom length *up* 5 inches (12.7 cm). Stitch the ends closed. Stitch at intervals to create pockets. Staple a 4-foot (1.22 m) length of yarn above pockets to tie around waist. Fold the top flap down one inch (2.54 cm). Label each pocket with something a soldier might have carried.

Mess Kettle

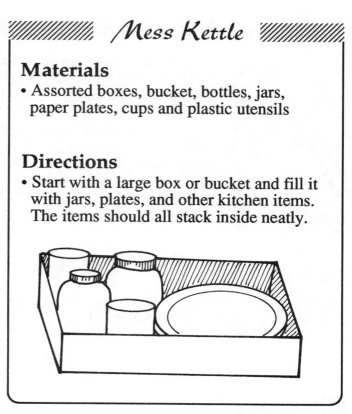

Materials
- Assorted boxes, bucket, bottles, jars, paper plates, cups and plastic utensils

Directions
- Start with a large box or bucket and fill it with jars, plates, and other kitchen items. The items should all stack inside neatly.

Canteen

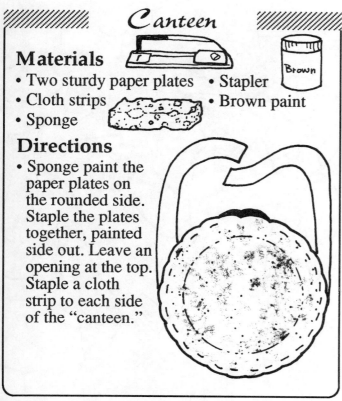

Materials
- Two sturdy paper plates
- Cloth strips
- Sponge
- Stapler
- Brown paint

Directions
- Sponge paint the paper plates on the rounded side. Staple the plates together, painted side out. Leave an opening at the top. Staple a cloth strip to each side of the "canteen."

Bullet-proof Vest

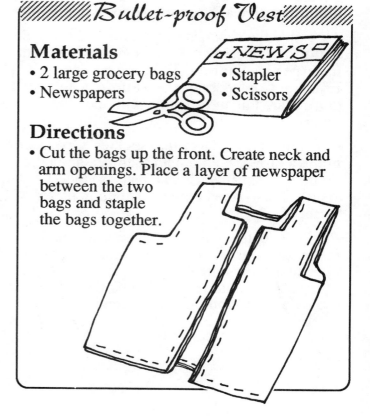

Materials
- 2 large grocery bags
- Newspapers
- Stapler
- Scissors

Directions
- Cut the bags up the front. Create neck and arm openings. Place a layer of newspaper between the two bags and staple the bags together.

Uniforms

Historical Aid

The official uniform for a Confederate soldier was a long gray shirt with light blue trousers and a gray flannel overcoat. Some wore shirts and pants of homespun cotton, dyed brown with walnut shells. Most wound up being dressed in scratchy wool shirts and roughly made pants.

Scores of regiments equipped themselves locally, wearing uniforms of their own design, financed by fund-raising drives or local businessmen. By the middle of the war, mismatched troops were a common sight, with deadly consequences when soldiers did not know who they were fighting on the battlefield.

Project

Create and dress in Civil War regiment uniforms and conduct a mock battle.

Materials

- Uniform Cards (following page)
- Materials as noted on the Uniform Cards
- Construction paper in eight colors
- Scissors
- Playground

Directions

1. Divide into eight groups. Cut apart the Uniform Cards and give a different one to each group.

2. Assemble the necessary materials and make the uniforms. On battle day, each group dresses in its respective uniform. Tell each group if it is Union or Confederate (see Uniform Cards), but don't share this information with the other groups.

3. Cut construction paper into squares. Give each group a different color and each person in the group four squares. Head outside to the "battlefield" armed with construction paper "weapons."

4. Begin the battle. Children give a construction paper square to a person they think is their opponent. When the battle is over, share the squares each child received in battle and evaluate if you fought foe or friend!

Union Uniforms

Artillery

The uniforms of Union artillery units changed as the war progressed. As soldiers became specialists in heavy artillery, their uniforms began to differ from infantrymen who carried lighter weapons.

Uniform
- Light blue pants
- Long, dark blue coat with red trim
- Black felt hat (similar to a cowboy hat) with red tassel
- Black leather waist and cross belts
- Brass shoulder trim and belt buckle

Sailors

The petty officers on Union ships were the ones who really ran the ship. They carried out the captain's orders and served as mate to all others on board. They wore much the same uniform as the common seamen.

Uniform
- Dark, baggy blue or white pants
- White shirts with large blue-striped collar and blue-striped cuffs
- Embroidered blue anchor on the shirt sleeve
- Blue sailor hat

Highlanders

One of the more colorful Union units was a group of Scottish immigrants from New York who formed an infantry unit known as the "Highlanders." Their dress kilts were usually changed before battle.

Uniform
- Plaid pants or kilts
- Blue jacket with red trim and gold shoulder decoration
- Red sash belt
- Silver-buckled shoes and sock garters
- Blue cloth kepi (hat) with blue band

Sharpshooters

Of the Union units known for their rifle skills, the most famous was Berdans Sharpshooters. These men were armed with the best weapons available and dressed in uniforms that would camouflage them.

Uniform
- Light blue or dark green pants and long jacket
- Black belt, brass buckle, black shoulder straps
- Canvas or leather leggings over boots
- Dark green cloth hat with red diamond in the center front

Confederate Uniforms

Cavalry

Cavalry units in the Confederacy were more informal. The Sussex Light Dragoons wore high-topped blue cloth kepis, trimmed with yellow braid and brass insignia. Enlisted men wore dark blue trousers and yellow shirts.

Uniform

- Dark blue pants
- Yellow or beige shirt with a panel in front
- Leather gloves
- Saber hung from the belt
- Blue cloth kepi (hat) with yellow lettering—SLD

Zoaves

Fancy uniforms patterned after French-Algerian zoaves were the rage for both armies, making it especially confusing on the battle field. The most prominent zoave force was a Confederate troop from Maryland.

Uniform

- Dark baggy blue trousers with red stripes
- Red shirts
- Blue jackets with red trim
- White canvas leggings
- Red cloth kepi (hat) with blue tassel

Sailors

Many who formed the crews on board fighting ships were adventurers from other nations. Discipline was lacking on some of the ships, but the men were required to wear regulation uniforms.

Uniform

- Gray shirts with white collar and cuffs
- Black tie around the collar
- Gray baggy pants
- White sash belt
- Black shoes
- Gray sailor hat

Infantry

Only a few Confederate infantry regiments got regulation uniforms, and that was very early in the war. Soldiers often had to replace their own uniforms, which varied in color and quality.

Uniform

- Dark gray or brown pants and vest
- Dark gray or brown coat; black stand-up collar and cuffs and gold braid sleeve trim; brass buttons
- Tan shirt, socks
- Canvas or leather leggings over boots
- Gray cloth kepi (hat)

Uniforms

The dwindling supply of uniforms, particularly among the Rebel forces, led to soldiers wearing whatever uniform they could get their hands on. Often they stripped a dead soldier for his shirt, trousers, shoes, and other articles of clothing. Much trading went on among the men in order to find a uniform that would fit.

Match Game

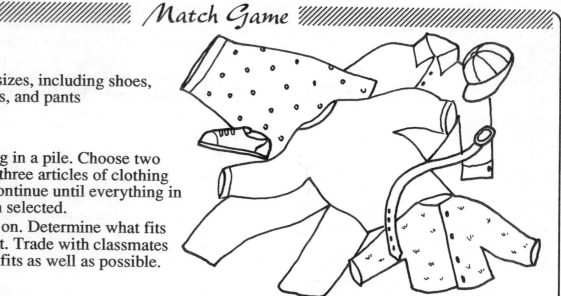

Supplies

• Clothing in all sizes, including shoes, belts, hats, shirts, and pants

Activity

• Place all clothing in a pile. Choose two people to select three articles of clothing from the pile. Continue until everything in the pile has been selected.

• Put the clothing on. Determine what fits and what doesn't. Trade with classmates until everything fits as well as possible.

The aid societies and others on the home front were faced with the prospects of making uniforms for the fighting troops from limited supplies. They had to be imaginative with their use of materials, recycling such things as curtains into articles of clothing that were useful to soldiers on the war front.

Recycling

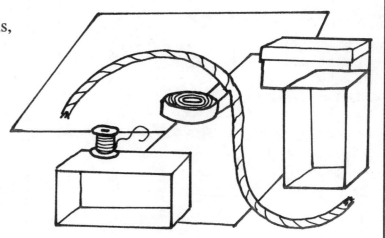

Supplies

• Discarded cloth items: sheets, rags, towels, pot holders, fabric

• Masking tape, thread, string, rope, cardboard, shoe boxes, and other recyclable materials

Activity

• Recycle the available materials to create a new article of clothing such as shoes, hat, belt or other item that might be worn by a soldier.

Camp Portraits

Historical Aid

Traveling photographers followed the troops from one battle site and encampment to the next, recording the events of the war. Soldiers paid about one dollar each for portraits to send home to loved ones. One of the first methods of photographic print was called a *daguerreotype*, named for Louis Daguerre, who perfected the process of exposing a silver copper plate to chemicals to create permanent images with outstanding detail.

In another method, an individual's photo image was printed from a glass negative onto a paper card. These small cards were called *carte de visite*. A soldier could purchase a dozen *carte de visite* for between three to five dollars.

Project

Create two types of camp portraits.

Materials

- Camp portrait projects (following page)
- Materials for each project, as listed

Directions

1. Review the project directions.

2. Divide into cooperative groups to paint the backdrops and from groups for regimental pictures. You may wish to remain in the groups formed for the different uniforms.

Camp Portraits

Daguerreotype

Materials
- Butcher paper
- Tempera paint
- Paint brushes
- Camera with black and white film
- Uniforms (see pages 24-27)
- Civil War reference books

Directions
- Review photographs from Civil War encampment.
- Paint a large mural "backdrop" featuring weaponry, tents, landscape and other images representative of camp life.
- Dress up in class-created uniforms and have "regiment" pictures taken against the backdrop.

Carte de Visite

Materials
- Six index cards
- Small personal photograph (school portrait size)
- Glue
- Photocopy machine

Directions
- Make six photocopies of each individual photo.
- Glue a photocopy to each index card to create six *carte de visite*.
- Include a signature and a brief message from the "war front."
- Trade the *carte de visite* with classmates.

Tents and Shelters

Historical Aid

The tent was a soldier's home for three seasons of the year. A variety appeared at the outset of the war. Some units came with candy-striped tents. Others showed up with nothing at all. Canvas tents, shaped like a small house, were popular, but were expensive and cumbersome to pitch and carry. They eventually became shelters for hospital patients and officers. The Sibley tent resembled a teepee, a tall cone of canvas supported by a center pole. Often more than twenty men inhabited a single tent, their heads at the outer rim and feet at the center pole. The dog tent, shaped like an upside-down V with rifles serving as poles, was most used by the soldiers. Two men each carried half, and they buttoned the halves together at night.

Project

Erect tents and create a mini war front encampment.

Materials

- Small sticks or tent stakes
- Dowels, broom handles, or long branches
- Sheets or other large pieces of material
- Scissors
- Tape
- Rope
- Hammer

Directions

1. Divide into groups of four.

2. Discuss the supplies needed to construct a tent. Use the material list as a guide. Assign each group member a material to supply.

3. Erect the tent shelters on a grassy area on the playground.

4. Evaluate the ease with which the tents were erected; how comfortable they might be to sleep in; and how effective they would be as protection against the weather.

5. Conduct some camp activities while the tents are constructed. Play games (see Camp Recreation, page 37) or eat a simple meal (see Battleground Food, page 34).

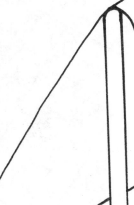

Housewife

Historical Aid

Newly enlisted soldiers, tempted by the large variety of items offered for sale, often took heavy packs along with them when they joined their company. It wasn't long before these "extras" were abandoned. Veteran soldiers traveled lightly, carrying few extra items. One of the most important was called a *housewife*, a small sewing kit stocked with needle, thread and buttons.

A housewife was essential on the war front. Men who had never used a needle and thread before became experts at patching rips, mending tears, and sewing on buttons. Replacement clothing was a rarity, particularly in the Southern states. Soldiers had to make "do" with the clothes on their backs.

Project

Make a "housewife" and learn the fundamentals of sewing.

Materials
- Needles
- Thread
- Scissors
- Fabric remnants
- Buttons

Directions

1. Practice threading the needle and tying a knot in the thread.

2. Cut one large rectangle and one smaller square of fabric to be sewn on as a pocket.

3. Place the pocket on the larger rectangle and use a running stitch on three sides to sew it in place.

4. Practice sewing on several buttons and some small patches, as well.

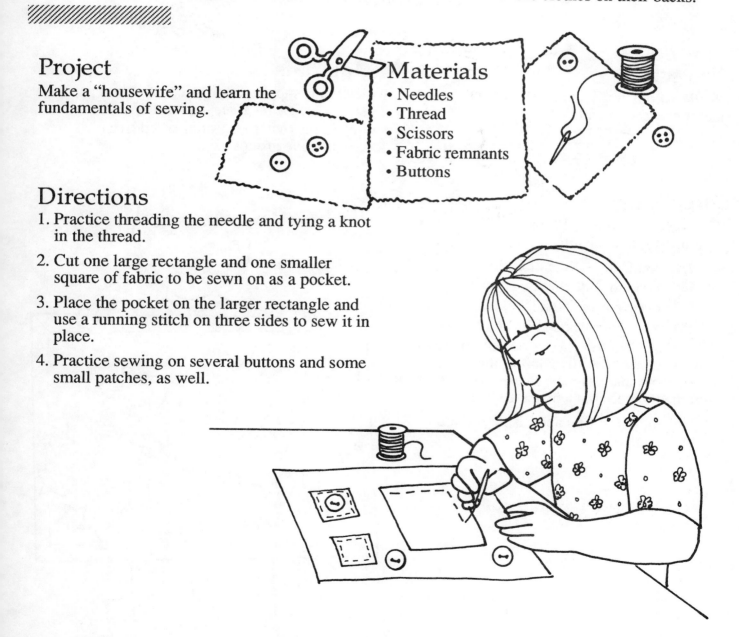

Regimental Flags

Historical Aid

When the various troops marched off to war, they carried with them the colors and insignia of their native state. Some flags carried their unit's nickname, like the Bartow Yankee Killers and Floyd Rangers. The flags were not uniform in design. They were sewn from silk, cotton, and wool. Some were made using the fabric of wedding dresses or grain sacks.

Despite its being the most dangerous post, men would vie with one another to carry the regimental banners into battle. As soon as one color bearer fell, another rushed to take his place. As many as a dozen or more men might fall carrying the colors in a single battle.

Project

Work in cooperative groups to design and make a regimental flag.

Materials

- Basic art supplies such as construction paper scraps, scissors, glue, stapler
- Available materials as requested by cooperative groups

Directions

1. Form cooperative groups. Discuss and make some group decisions:

   - Are you Confederate or Union?
   - From which state do you come?
   - What is your troop's nickname?
   - What are your troop colors?

2. Design a flag for your regiment. Decide on the material from which it will be made, then assign people to locate in class or bring from home the necessary materials.

3. Construct your flag and display it in the classroom.

Buglers and Drummers

Historical Aid

Most soldiers were between eighteen and twenty-nine years old. Sixteen- and seventeen-year-olds who wanted to enlist wrote the number "18" on slips of paper and put them in their shoes. When asked by a recruiting officer how old they were, they could say, "over eighteen." Ten- and 12-year-olds often were placed in the supposedly non-combatant roles of buglers and drummers. The youngest soldier of the war, aged nine, joined as a musician.

Drum rolls and bugle calls stood for certain orders. There were fifteen general drum and twenty-six bugle calls, and more for skirmishes. Forgetting their meaning could prove disastrous for a fighting man.

Project

Respond to commands issued by drum and whistle rhythms.

Materials

- Drum and drumstick, or object on which to beat a rhythm
- Whistle
- Chalkboard, chalk

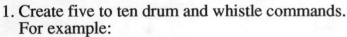

Directions

1. Create five to ten drum and whistle commands. For example:

   - Three drum beats: Step forward five paces.
   - Two whistle blasts and two drum beats: Lie down.

2. Spend some time memorizing the commands and their meanings.

3. Head outside to the "battlefield." Choose two children to be drummer and bugler. "Play" a command and ask classroom troops to follow. Allow time between each one. Change buglers and drummers occasionally. Evaluate your success!

Battlefield Food

Historical Aid

Near-famine conditions hampered troops on both sides. Union soldiers lived mainly on salt pork, bread, beans, and coffee, supplemented with cakes and pies bought from *sutlers*, peddlers who followed troops from camp to camp. Aid societies in the North sent thousands of boxes containing smoked meats, pies, dried fruits, and jams. Most of the food spoiled before it reached the troops.

Confederate supplies were not as plentiful. They suffered through days with no rations. Meals were fried in grease and stomach ailments abounded. *Hardtack*, rock-hard flour-and-water biscuits, were the main staple, but were so infested with insects that soldiers came to call them "worm-castles."

Project

Simulate a battlefield and dine on Civil War soldiers' rations.

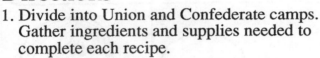

Materials

- Camp Recipes, following
- Hot plate
- Pans
- Bowls
- Plastic spoons
- Ingredients as listed in each recipe

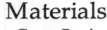

Directions

1. Divide into Union and Confederate camps. Gather ingredients and supplies needed to complete each recipe.

2. Set up a "chow" line in each camp.

3. Serve the meals and "coffee" (juice).

Battlefield Food

North

South

Salt Horse

A slang term for salted beef issued by the Northern army. So salty it lasted two years before decaying. Soldiers soaked it for hours before they could stand to eat it.

Ingredients
- Packaged beef jerky
- Water

Directions
1. Break beef jerky into small pieces.
2. Soak jerky in a bowl of water until softened.

Bully Soup

Northern hot cereal consisting of cornmeal, crushed hardtack, wine, ginger, and water, all cooked together.

Ingredients
- 1 cup (250 ml) corn meal
- 5 cups (1.18 l) water
- Saltine crackers, crumbled
- Ground ginger to taste

Directions
1. Combine cornmeal and 1 cup (250 ml) water in saucepan.
2. Add remaining ingredients and cook, stirring constantly, until thickened.

Cush

Confederate stew made with bacon, cornbread, and water, cooked until the water evaporated.

Ingredients
- Bacon, cooked and broken into small pieces
- Cornbread
- Water

Directions
1. Break cornbread into small pieces.
2. Combine bacon and cornbread with enough water to soak cornbread.

Artificial Oysters

Southern mixture of grated green corn mixed with egg and butter, then rolled and fried.

Ingredients

- 1 cup (250 ml) cream-style corn
- 2 eggs, beaten
- 6 Tbsp. (89 ml) flour
- ½ tsp. (2.46 ml) baking powder
- Butter for frying

Directions
1. Combine ingredients in bowl.
2. Drop by spoonfuls into butter in frying pan. Cook on one side until brown. Turn over and brown other side.

Medal of Honor

Historical Aid

Courageous acts abounded on the battlefield. The governments of the opposing forces devised ways to honor this bravery. Confederate fighting forces were recognized by a Roll of Honor published after every fight. The Union, which had had no military decorations since the Revolutionary War, established the *Medal of Honor* in 1861, with Congressional approval, to recognize acts of bravery. The approval caused much debate among U.S. citizens and politicians because many people considered medals symbols of European monarchies. Over one thousand Medals of Honor were awarded to Civil War soldiers, including at least twenty-one to black soldiers.

Project

Create a paper replica of a Civil War-era Medal of Honor.

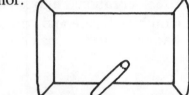

Directions

1. Reproduce the medal illustration on the chalkboard.

2. Create a construction paper Medal of Honor.

3. Use a safety pin to attach the medal to clothing.

Materials

- Red, white, blue, and brown construction paper
- Scissors
- Glue
- Safety pin
- Chalk and chalkboard

Camp Recreation

Historical Aid

For every day spent in battle, Yankees and Rebels passed weeks and months fighting other enemies: heat and cold, hunger, poor sanitation, and the monotony of drill, training, and camp life. Camp diversions included music and conversation around a campfire, checkers, chess, and card games. Some took up carving as a hobby, making poker chips, whistles, and small figurines out of wood and animal bone.

More active pastimes included wrestling and foot races, sometimes with wheelbarrows or over hurdles. Cannon balls were used as bowling balls with cricket pins as their targets. Baseball—a different version than today's—was often played.

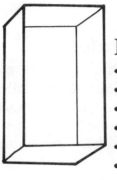

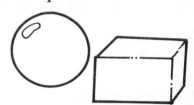

Project

Participate in indoor and outdoor camp recreational activities.

Materials

• Checker and chess board and pieces
• Playing cards
• Wood blocks
• Rubber ball
• Shoe boxes
• Baseball
• Hurdles

Directions

1. Set up three indoor recreation stations:

   • Checkers and chess

   • Card games

   • Wood construction—wood blocks and glue

2. Set up three outdoor recreation stations:

   • Bowling—upended shoe boxes, rubber ball

   • Hurdles

   • Baseball diamond and equipment

3. Plan a day (or as time permits) to participate in these activities. Children may rotate through all areas or choose those of interest.

Music

Historical Aid

In the military encampments and on the home front, each side rallied around music that became identified with their cause. Every camp had a band that featured instruments the soldiers carried from home, and any they could make from materials on hand. Sounds of fiddles, harmonicas, and banjos filled the air when weary soldiers gathered around a campfire. Those who didn't have instruments whistled tunes and sang.

Larger companies formed musical groups that performed for civilian and military personnel.

Project

Gather around a campfire and play some Civil War music.

Materials

- Brown butcher paper
- Song sheets, following
- Records or tapes containing songs listed on the Song Sheet
- Musical instruments
- Masking tape
- Tape or record player

Directions

1. Create a campfire by rolling and taping brown butcher paper into logs.

2. Clear an area for the "campfire" and stack the logs in the center.

3. Reproduce copies of the Song Sheet to hand out.

4. Bring musical instruments to the campfire and play, sing, or whistle along with the songs on the record or tape player.

Extended Activity

Many songs have an interesting history. The Battle Hymn of the Republic was originally a poem written by Julia Ward Howe, a citizen who was inspired after viewing a grand review of the troops in Washington, D.C. Research the history of other patriotic and Civil War songs.

Song Sheet

North

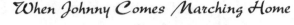

Union musical favorites included:
When Johnny Comes Marching Home; The Battle Hymn of the Republic; John Brown's Body; Rally Round the Flag; Tenting on the Old Campground

The Battle Hymn of the Republic

Mine eyes have seen the glory of the
  coming of the Lord,
He is trampling out the vintage where the
  grapes of wrath are stored;
He has loosed the fateful lightning of His
  terrible swift sword,
His truth is marching on!

When Johnny Comes Marching Home

When Johnny comes marching home
  again, hurrah, hurrah!
We'll give him a hearty welcome then,
  hurrah, hurrah!
The men will cheer, the boys will shout,
  the ladies they will all turn out,
And we'll all feel gay when Johnny comes
  marching home.

South

Confederate musical favorites included:
Bonnie Blue Flag; Home Sweet Home; Dixie; Pop Goes the Weasel; Shoo Fly Shoo; Goober Peas

Goober Peas

Sitting by the road side on a
  summer day,
Chatting with my messmates
  passing time away;
Lying in the shadow
  underneath the trees,
Goodness how delicious,
  eating goober peas.
Peas, peas, peas, peas, eating
  goober peas,
Goodness how delicious,
  eating goober peas.

Dixie

I wish I was in the land of cotton,
Old times there are not forgotten,
Look away, look away, look away Dixie
  land.
In Dixie land where I was born in
Early on one frosty mornin',
Look away, look away, look away Dixie
  land.
Then I wish I was in Dixie, hooray, hooray.
In Dixie land I'll take my stand
To live and die in Dixie,
Away, away, away down south in Dixie.
Away, away, away down south in Dixie.

Newspapers

Historical Aid

Much of the news from the war front consisted of rumors. The most dependable source of information was the newspaper. Even the spies on both sides turned to enemy newspapers for information. The North had more paper mills and printing presses, and therefore had more newspapers and reporters.

As the war progressed, paper became scarce, particularly in the Confederate states. They wrote on scraps of paper. When they ran out of newsprint, they printed on the back of patterned wallpaper, brown wrapping paper, and thin tissue paper. When supplies of ink were gone, they used shoe polish. By the end of the war, only twenty Southern newspapers remained.

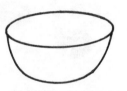

Project

Create a newspaper using different kinds of paper.

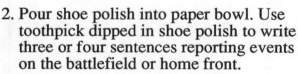
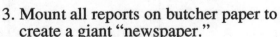

Materials

- Wallpaper samples
- Tissue paper
- Brown bags or wrapping paper
- Shoe polish
- Paper bowl
- Toothpicks
- Butcher paper

Directions

1. Select paper—wallpaper, tissue paper, or brown paper.

2. Pour shoe polish into paper bowl. Use toothpick dipped in shoe polish to write three or four sentences reporting events on the battlefield or home front.

3. Mount all reports on butcher paper to create a giant "newspaper."

Correspondents

Historical Aid

In the early years of the war, the Pony Express carried news reports. However, a year after the war began, reporters traveling with troops were able to send their reports via telegraph. Their average salary was $25 per week. The invention of photography twenty-two years earlier made the Civil War the first war to be recorded with photo-journalism. Some newspapers also paid illustrators to sketch battlefield scenes and impressions.

Small towns couldn't afford to pay correspondents. They filled their newspapers with letters mailed from soldiers, and reprints of stories from larger papers.

Project

Create a war correspondent's sketch book.

Materials
- Pens and pencils
- Drawing paper
- Butcher paper

Directions

1. Use pens, pencils, and drawing paper to make sketches of Civil War battle or war front scenes.

2. Mount sketches on butcher paper to make a bulletin board display. Articles describing the sketches may also be included.

The Presidents

Jefferson Davis

Jefferson Davis, as president of the Confederate States of America, came to be the symbol for the convictions of the South. Davis was an experienced statesman, serving as a Democrat in the U.S. House of Representatives and the U.S. Senate. He made many improvements for the armed forces as secretary of war under President Franklin Pierce. Davis had a distinguished military career, serving in the Black Hawk Wars. He was a serious student of the Constitution and political philosophy.

Davis was elected to the provisional presidency of the Confederacy in February, 1861, and to the presidency in 1862. He was not a popular leader, criticized by many Southerners for his running of the war. However, he gained the respect of many during his imprisonment after the war, and his lifelong defense of the Southern cause made him a symbol of the South's ideals.

Abraham Lincoln

Abraham Lincoln's greatest cause during the Civil War was to keep the nation united. Born on the American frontier and largely self-educated, he had a tremendous belief that whether slavery was abolished or not, one strong nation was far better than two weaker nations. As a young man, Lincoln served briefly in the military during the Black Hawk War. He worked at several careers: storekeeper, postmaster, surveyor, and finally lawyer. He served four terms in the Illinois legislature, and one term in the U.S. House of Representatives as a Whig. In 1856 he joined the two-year-old antislavery Republican party, and became an influential speaker on the party's behalf. As presidential nominee in 1860, Lincoln won the presidency with less than 40 percent of the popular vote.

Lincoln's election was the trigger that caused the first of the Southern states to secede from the Union, precipitating the start of the Civil War. Many of Lincoln's war-time policies were unpopular. He was the chief architect of the Union's military strategy and he was often in conflict with his own military leaders. Lincoln took a personal interest in the people involved in the war, and took time to see widows and children of his soldiers. By the time of his second election in 1864, the war had taken a dreadful toll on his health and strength. On April 14, 1865, five days after Lee's surrender to Grant, Lincoln was assassinated.

Jefferson Davis and Abraham Lincoln became symbols for the South and the North, as well as for the ideals of the divided nation. Flags were the other great symbol for each group, soldiers vying for the honor of carrying their banners bravely into battle.

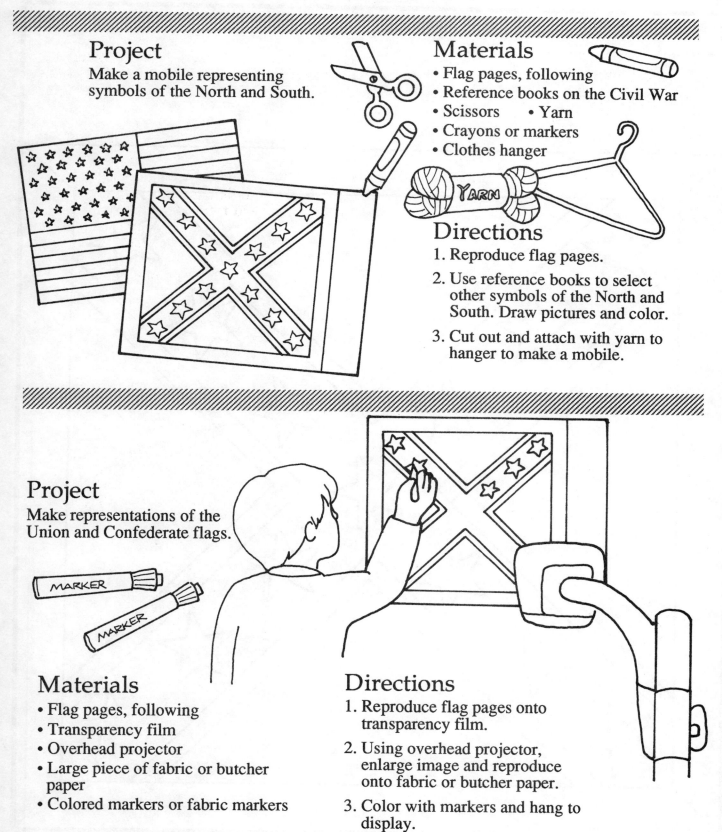

Project

Make a mobile representing symbols of the North and South.

Materials

- Flag pages, following
- Reference books on the Civil War
- Scissors • Yarn
- Crayons or markers
- Clothes hanger

Directions

1. Reproduce flag pages.

2. Use reference books to select other symbols of the North and South. Draw pictures and color.

3. Cut out and attach with yarn to hanger to make a mobile.

Project

Make representations of the Union and Confederate flags.

Materials

- Flag pages, following
- Transparency film
- Overhead projector
- Large piece of fabric or butcher paper
- Colored markers or fabric markers

Directions

1. Reproduce flag pages onto transparency film.

2. Using overhead projector, enlarge image and reproduce onto fabric or butcher paper.

3. Color with markers and hang to display.

Confederate Flag

Union Flag

General Sherman

Historical Aid

William Tecumseh Sherman was one of the most prominent generals of the Union army. He commanded forces at the Battles of Bull Run and Shiloh, and took part in the capture of Vicksburg. In 1864, he came under the command of Ulysses S. Grant, who appointed Sherman the commander of Union forces in the West.

With three armies totalling 100,000 men, he captured Atlanta, and then began his famous "March to the Sea." His entire army marched across Georgia, destroying the last of the South's economic resources. With Georgia conquered, Sherman then moved through South Carolina. Waging an economic war against the civilians of the South made Sherman the first modern general.

Project

Research Sherman's march across Georgia and South Carolina. Create a map outlining the route.

Materials

- Reference books
- U.S. map
- Butcher paper
- Pencils
- Markers

Directions

1. Use reference books to create a written outline of Sherman's route.

2. Use U.S. map to recreate a map of the area covered, including details like mountains, bodies of water, and cities.

3. Trace Sherman's path, marking the progress with available dates.

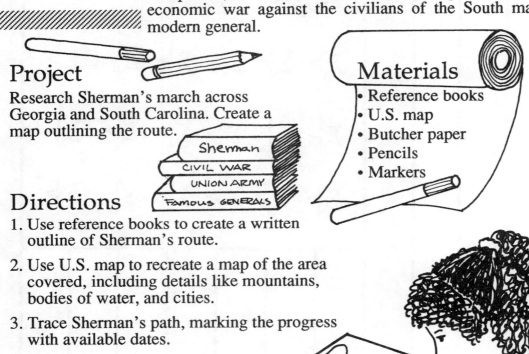

Robert E. Lee

Historical Aid

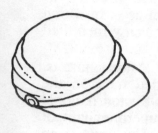

Robert E. Lee was one of the great generals of the Confederacy, but he was admired greatly by both the North and the South. His father was a famous cavalry leader in the Revolutionary War. Lee graduated with honors from West Point, and had a distinguished military career.

When his home state of Virginia seceded from the Union, Lee faced a dilemma. He did not believe in secession, but could not fight against family and friends. He took charge of the Army of Virginia, even though Lincoln had asked him to head the Union army. Forced to surrender to General Grant on April 9, 1865, Lee represented the Southern troops with honor, in full dress uniform, complete with sword.

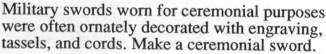

Project

Military swords worn for ceremonial purposes were often ornately decorated with engraving, tassels, and cords. Make a ceremonial sword.

Materials

- Poster board
- Cardboard bowls
- Scissors
- Glue
- Tape
- Heavy yarn or cord
- Aluminum foil

Directions

1. Cut sword blade from poster board.

2. Cut slit in bottom of bowl and insert end of blade, adjusting so that bowl becomes a handle covering hand. Tape into place.

3. Glue yarn in a pattern to outside of handle.

4. Cover handle with foil, pressing carefully and firmly to show ridges of yarn pattern through foil.

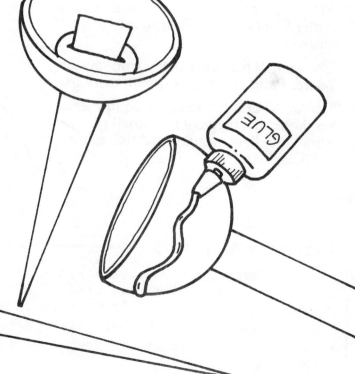

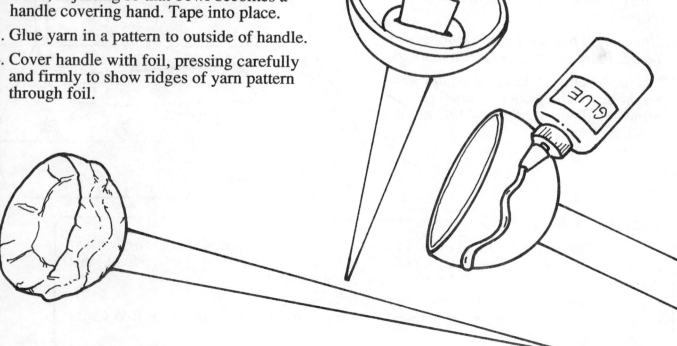

Clara Barton

Historical Aid

Medical care for the men wounded on Civil War battlefields was primitive. Medical equipment was often not cleaned between uses. Infection in wounds was common because there were no antibiotics. Many men died from infectious diseases caused by poor sanitation.

Clara Barton, a government clerk from North Oxford, Massachusetts, began to carry supplies to soldiers, and to nurse wounded men on the battlefield. Called the *Angel of the Battlefield*, her work attracted national attention and appreciation. In 1864, she was appointed superintendent of nurses for the Army of the James. After the Civil War, she formed an organization to search for missing men.

Project

Gather equipment to be used in a medical kit on a Civil War battlefield.

Materials

- Shoe box
- Muslin
- Poster board
- Scissors
- Markers
- Black tempera paint and brush
- Needles and thread, small pliers (optional)

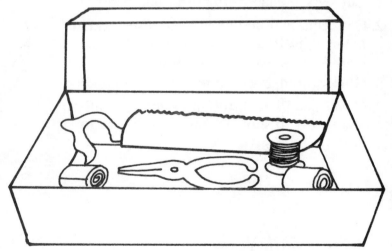

Directions

1. Paint shoe box.

2. Make bandages by cutting muslin into 3-inch (7.5 cm) strips. Roll tightly and store in box.

3. Cut a small handsaw shape from poster board. Paint or embellish with markers.

4. Decide what other kinds of equipment might be in a medical kit (small pliers to remove bullets, needles and thread for stitches).

Extended Activity

Clara Barton is also known as the founder of the American Red Cross. She learned of the International Committee of the Red Cross while visiting Switzerland, and became the first president of the American Branch in 1881.

- Research the history of the Red Cross organization.
- Look through newspapers and magazines to determine what things the Red Cross does today.